15

Wonderful
Writing Prompt
Mini-Books

**Reproducible Mini-Books With Instant Prompts and Story Frames
That Invite Kids to Write About Themselves and Create Fun Stories**

by Betsy Franco

SCHOLASTIC
PROFESSIONAL BOOKS

New York • Toronto • London • Auckland • Sydney
Mexico City • New Delhi • Hong Kong • Buenos Aires

For the children of
El Carmelo School,
who give me "writing
prompts" every morning
just by being themselves.

Cover design by **Josué Castilleja**
Cover and interior artwork by **Paige Billin-Frye**
Interior design by **BHG Graphic Designs**

ISBN: 0439-26277-1
Copyright © 2001 by **Scholastic, Inc.**
All rights reserved.
Printed in the U.S.A.

Contents

The Mini-Books

Introduction

Writing will flow freely from children with *15 Wonderful Writing Prompt Mini-Books*! These make-your-own books are fun, engaging, relevant, and carefully crafted for young writers. As children complete each of the 15 books in the set, they will be engaged in writing, reading, oral literacy, and art. Children will create little books that are so personal and charming, they will surely become family keepsakes for years to come! Children will have a variety of writing experiences:

☆ Some of the mini-books encourage children to write about their feelings, their families and friends, their favorite things, and their school.

☆ Some awaken children's imaginations as they write silly stories and tall tales about such things as babysitting for a gorilla! In *Animal Tales*, they describe what it might be like to swim like a fish or fly like an eagle.

☆ Holidays come into play in the books *Happy Valentine's Day!* and *I'm Thankful!*

☆ Children are also given a chance to write their own fairy tales and to write letters to favorite fairy tale characters. For example, they'll give a few helpful suggestions to Goldilocks and the Big Bad Wolf!

Using the Mini-Books in Your Classroom

Depending on ability and developmental level, children will respond to the prompts in different ways. Some will answer in one word or sentence, while others will take the prompt and "run with it." These simple steps will help you and your class get the most from each book:

1. Explain to children that they will be writing their very own books and show an assembled book to the class. Discuss how several authors can write about the same topic and come up with a completely different book — this is what keeps libraries and bookstores full! Emphasize that each child is an author with his or her very own stories to tell.

2. For every book, photocopy the pages for each child and model the assembly of the books as children follow your lead (see right).

3. Discuss the title and the topic of each book. On pages 6–8, you'll find specific suggestions for getting started. These introductory brainstorming and discussion sessions will clarify the task and inspire children to write.

4. Go through each book page by page so children understand what information and illustrations they will be contributing.

5. Give children time to complete and color their books. Explain that this is an opportunity to tell about themselves or to use their limitless imaginations! Encourage them to write as much as they can.

6. Sharing the books is an important final step. Children will strengthen their oral literacy, and the experience will validate their writing attempts as others listen to their feelings, opinions, and ideas. Children can share with the whole class, in small groups, with a partner, or with an older buddy. Finally, taking the books home helps families become involved with the growing literacy of their children.

How to Assemble the Mini-Books

The books have been designed for ease of assembly. It is best to assemble the books together as a class—you might assemble and complete one yourself to use as a model when introducing the book.

1. Copy the pages for books on standard 8 1/2- by 11-inch paper, making the pages double-sided.

2. Fold each page in half along the dashed lines.

3. Place the pages in number order and staple along the spine.

For the smaller mini-books
(see pages 57–60)
1. Copy the page onto standard 8 1/2- by 11-inch paper, making the pages double-sided.

2. Cut each sheet into four small pages and arrange in number order. Staple.

If desired, children can create additional protective covers with construction paper.

Creating the Mini-Books

Page 9

My Book About Feelings
Children label and elaborate upon different feelings.
Introduce the Book: Have children name as many feeling words as they can. Record their contributions on chart paper. You might discuss how children are feeling that day or help them recall situations that have made them happy, sad, mad, or scared.
Make the Book: Help children assemble the book and invite them to write about situations that cause them to feel certain ways, then color each page.

Page 13

All About Me
Children experience the genre of autobiography.
Introduce the Book: Show children the cover and explain that this type of book is called an autobiography.
Make the Book: Let children illustrate and complete each page. Point out illustrations when they appear, and encourage children to use them to spark ideas.

Page 17

The Friendly Monster
Children narrate a full-length piece of fiction.
Introduce the Book: Discuss with children what it might be like to have a pet monster! What might they name their monster?
Make the Book: Children complete each sentence with their ideas about what the monster might do in the various settings, and then color in and add to the illustrations.

Page 21

I'm Thankful!
Patterned, predictable text helps children reflect on Thanksgiving.
Introduce the Book: Discuss the meaning of the word "thankful" and have children list things for which they are thankful. Record responses on chart paper.
Make the Book: Children can color and complete each page. This little book makes a perfect Thanksgiving gift for families!

Page 25

My Favorite Things
Children extend the autobiography experience.
Introduce the Book: Talk about the concept of "favorites." Ask each child to name a favorite ice cream flavor, favorite color, and so on.
Make the Book: Children complete and illustrate or color each page.

Animal Tales

Children take flights of fancy in an imaginative mini-book.

Introduce the Book: Ask children which animal they would be if they could be any animal, and have them explain why.

Make the Book: Children complete sentences and color each page. Explain that the sky's the limit and that they can write anything they imagine!

Page 29

Silly Stories

Open-ended fictional prompts springboard children into the worlds of fantasy and tall tales.

Introduce the Book: Brainstorm with the writing prompt on the first page about a child who looks at him or herself in the mirror and exclaims, "Oh, no!" Let the class imagine what provoked the exclamation.

Make the Book: Point out the dedication page and explain what a dedication is. On each page, children use the picture and sentence starters as writing prompts.

Page 33

School Days

Perfect for open houses, this mini-book invites children to describe and illustrate their school experience.

Introduce the Book: Ask children what they like to learn, what their favorite places in school are, and so on.

Make the Book: Children complete the sentences and color or illustrate each page. You might point out page 7, on which they describe a funny thing that happened at school (remind them that this should be something that was funny for everyone, not something embarrassing to one child!)

Page 37

The 100th Day of School

Children enrich their "100th Day of School" experience with this creative mini-book!

Introduce the Book: Use this book on the 100th day of school. Start by asking questions such as: What food would you like to eat 100 of?

Make the Book: Children color and complete each page. Encourage them to explain their reasons for their choices.

Page 41

The Lonely Giant

Children narrate a full short story from beginning to end.

Introduce the Book: Discuss situations in which children feel lonely. Have them speculate as to why a giant might be lonely (for instance, he doesn't physically fit anywhere, everyone is afraid of him, and so on).

Make the Book: Children color in the illustrations on each page and use the writing prompts to complete the story. Point out that the last page is "About the Author," and help them decide what information to include about themselves.

Page 45

My Words of Wisdom

Children take an imaginative trip into both the fairy tale and the letter-writing genres.

Introduce the Book: Quickly review the story of Cinderella or Rapunzel and together, write a collaborative letter with suggestions to either character. For instance, children might suggest to Rapunzel that she start doing exercises so that she can escape by climbing down the outside of the tower.

Make the Book: Children can compose their own letter on each page and color the illustrations. On the last page of this book, children can correspond with any character from a favorite story.

Happy Valentine's Day!

Infuse this holiday with literacy by creating colorful, descriptive valentine books.

Introduce the Book: Discuss the meaning of Valentine's Day. You might also share different Valentine's Day cards with the group.

Make the Book: Go through the book with the group, pointing out what the children might write and draw on each page. *Happy Valentine's Day!* will make a lovely gift for families!

My Buggy Book

Children explore a popular, colorful science topic in a non-fiction mini-book.

Introduce the Book: Have each child contribute one word that comes to mind when they think of bugs.

Make the Book: Children illustrate and complete each page. Point out the last page, on which they will make up an imaginary bug and describe it.

My Dream World

Children describe a world of limitless possibilities.

Introduce the Book: Talk about the concept of a "dream world." Explain to children that dreams do not only happen when we're asleep, but the word can mean "something we really want to do or have."

Make the Book: Children complete and illustrate each page. Help them brainstorm ideas for page 8, on which they make up their own "dream" idea.

My Very Own Folk and Fairy Tales

Children put their own spin on myths, legends, and folk and fairy tales with rich and inviting writing prompts.

Introduce the Book: Explain that some stories, such as the one they will write on page 4 and 6, are called "pourquoi tales," or stories that explain why things are a certain way.

Make the Book: So that children get the idea of the mini-book, brainstorm ideas for the first fairy tale. Children can then begin writing their own fairy tales and coloring the illustrations.

My Book About Feelings

by _____

Here's what makes me scared:

_____
_____
_____
_____
_____

4

Here's what makes me happy:

2

Here's what makes me sad:

3

And here's the very best feeling
that I've ever had:

Here's what makes me laugh
(it really makes me glad!):

shocked · delighted · nervous · tickled · grumpy · joyful · upset · worried · silly · goofy · thankful · jealous · embarrassed · surprised

Now I've told my feelings
from mad to sad to glad.
And here is one last feeling
that I would like to add:

I feel _____

when _____

_____

_____

_____

8

Here's what
makes me mad:

_____

_____

_____

_____

_____

5

All About Me

by _____

I like to

_____
_____
_____
_____
_____
_____
_____

4

My Autograph

My full name is

_____

I like to be called

_____

2

Here is a picture of me.
This is what I look like:

_____

_____

_____

_____

3

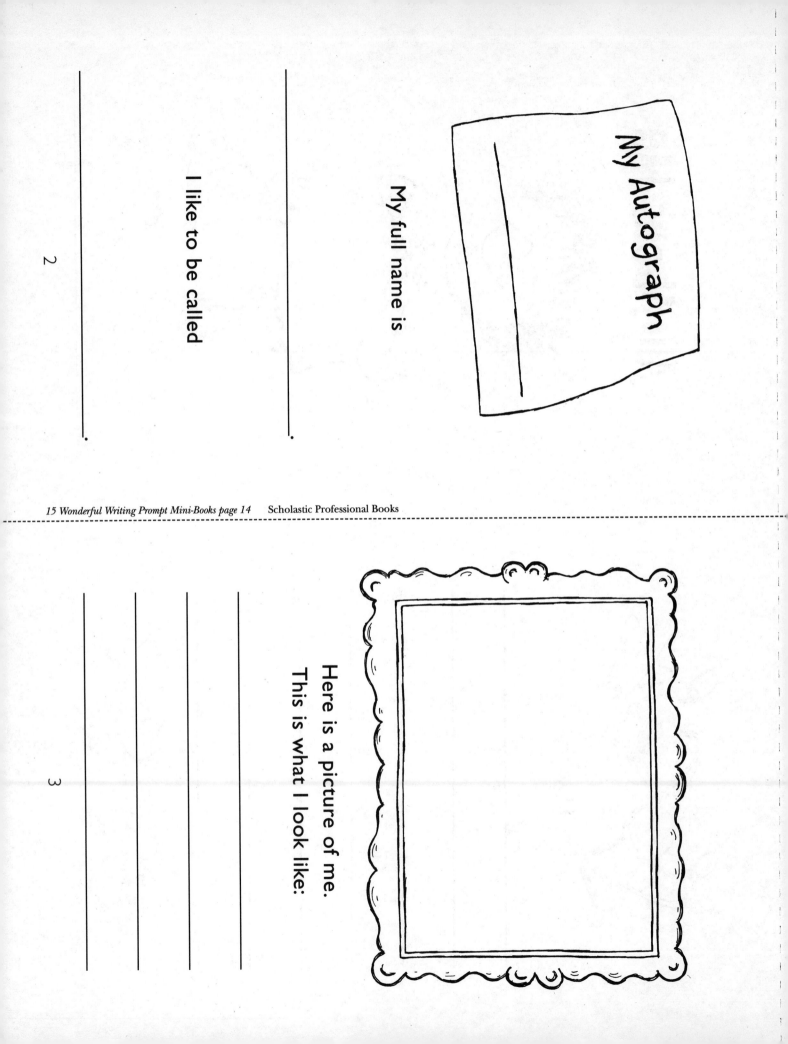

I have some ideas about what
I'd like to be when I grow up:

7

If my friend described me,
he or she might say that I was

6

If I could change one thing about the world, I would change _____

The one thing I would never change about me is _____

8

These are the people in my family.
Let me tell you about them:

5

The Friendly Monster

by _____

Monster was afraid of the daylight.
I took its hand and I told it

"_____
_____
_____
_____"

4

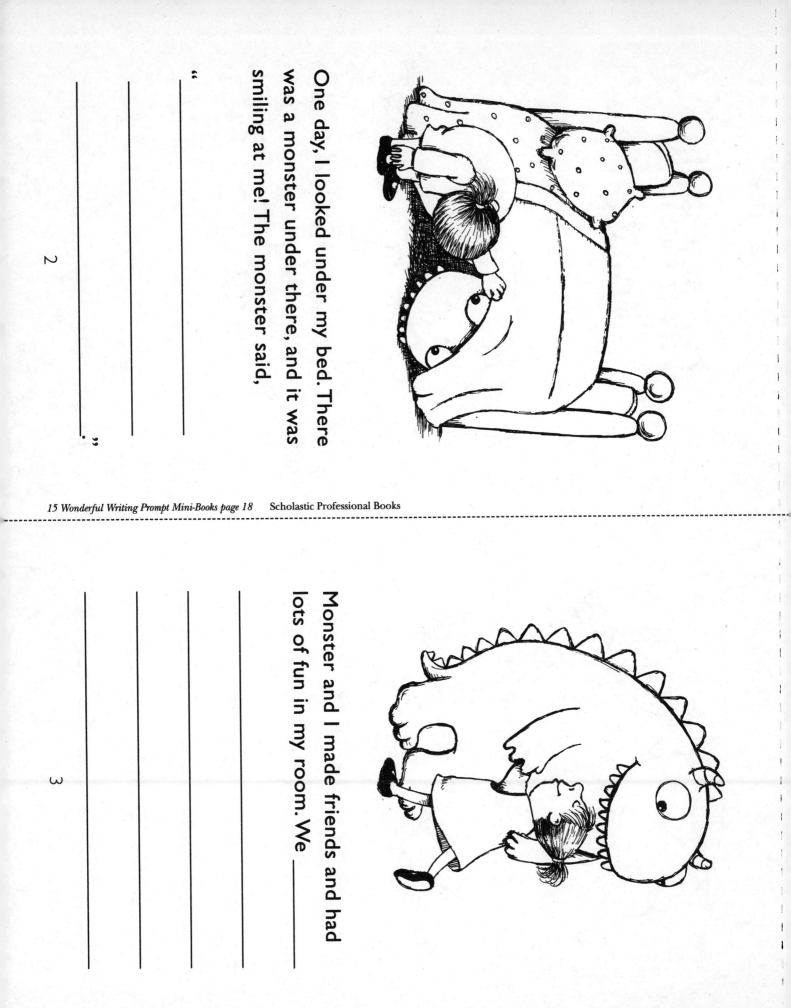

One day, I looked under my bed. There was a monster under there, and it was smiling at me! The monster said,

"_____
_____
_____
_____."

2

Monster and I made friends and had lots of fun in my room. We _____
_____
_____
_____
_____

3

When we were at recess, all the kids started laughing because Monster

7

Monster came to school with me. As soon as it walked into the classroom,

6

In the classroom, the teacher was surprised when Monster _____ _____ _____ .

But my teacher let Monster stay all day!

8

The first person Monster met was _____ who said, " _____ _____ _____ . "

5

I'm Thankful!

by _____

At mealtimes, I'm thankful for _____

_____

_____

_____

_____

4

On Thanksgiving, I'm thankful for

2

I'm thankful for my family because

3

I'm thankful I have

_____

_____

_____

_____

_____

7

Outside, when I look at nature, I'm thankful for

_____

_____

_____

_____

6

I almost forgot! I'm also thankful for

8

At school, I'm thankful for

5

My Favorite Things

by _____

And here's a book I really, really liked to read:

4

This little book is all about me. It's all about my favorite things and what I like to do. Here I am in my favorite place. My favorite place is:

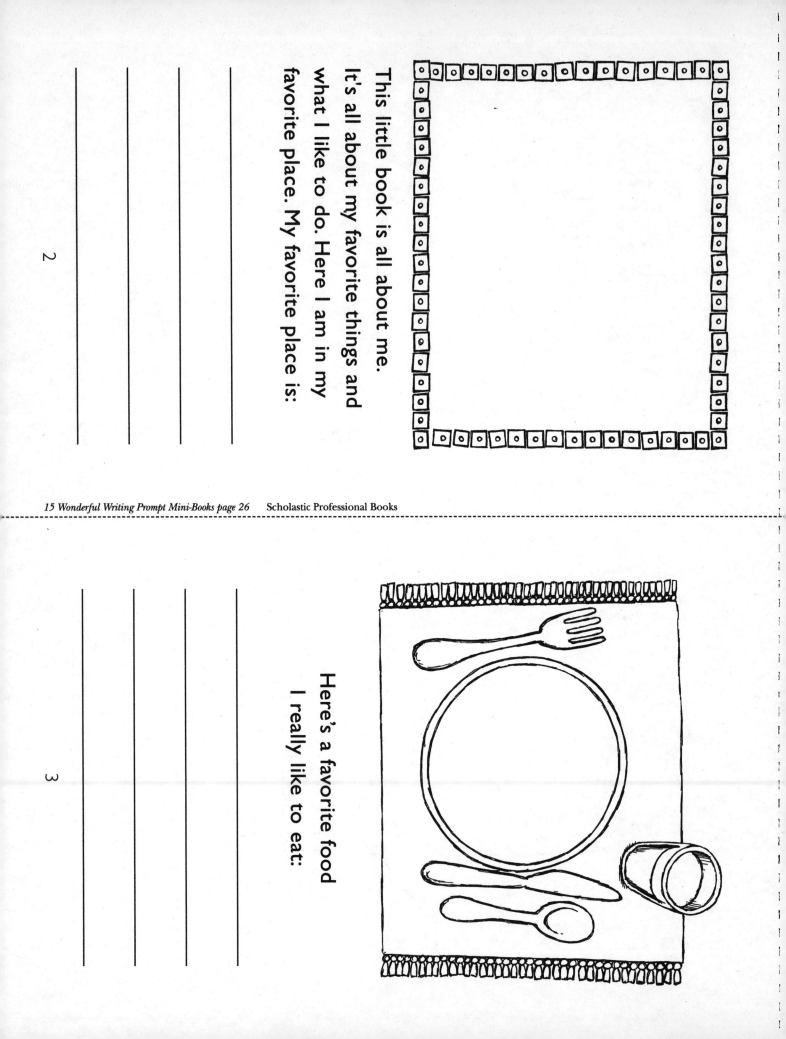

2

Here's a favorite food I really like to eat:

3

When I get dressed for school,
here's my favorite thing to wear:

_____

_____

_____

_____

7

And here's my favorite pet
if I could have most any sort:

_____

_____

_____

6

And here's the place I'd visit
if I could go anywhere!

8

Let me tell you about my favorite
game or my favorite sport.

5

Animal Tales

by _____

If I were as tiny as an ant, I would

_____

_____

_____

_____

_____

4

If I could swim like a fish, I would

2

If I had wings like an eagle, I would

3

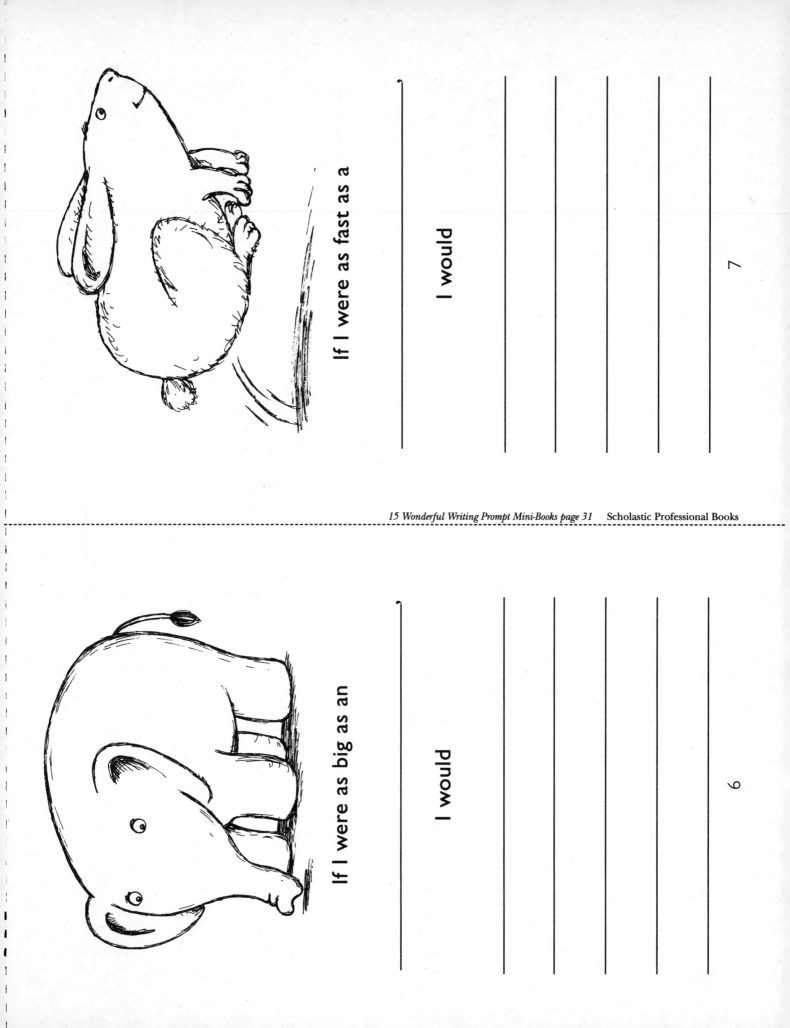

If I were as fast as a

I would

_____

_____

_____

_____

_____

7

If I were as big as an

I would

_____

_____

_____

_____

_____

6

My favorite animal is the _____.

If I could be like my favorite animal,
I would _____

_____

_____

_____

_____

8

If I could climb like a monkey, I would

_____

_____

_____

_____

5

Which bug
really bugs you?

_____

Why? _____

_____

_____

_____

5

Which bug would make
a pretty good pet?

_____

Why? _____

_____

_____

_____

4

Scholastic Professional Books

8

My Buggy Book

by _____

I

If you could be any bug, which bug would you be?

_____

Why? _____

_____

_____

3

Color this bug from its head to its toes.

6

Which of these bugs have you seen outside?

_____

_____

_____

ladybug
bee
fly
spider
grasshopper
beetle
ant

2

Now describe a bug that nobody knows! This bug _____

_____

_____

_____

7

Silly Stories

by _____

On Tuesday, I had to babysit a gorilla.

What a day! _____

_____

_____

_____

_____

4

This book is dedicated to

_____

who makes me laugh.
Here are some silly stories
to make you laugh!

2

On Monday, I woke up and looked
in the mirror. "Oh, no!" I yelled.

3

On Wednesday, a _____ got loose in our classroom!

_____

_____

_____

_____

_____

5

And on Saturday, the silliest thing of all happened. I was reading a book

about _____,

when suddenly I was inside the book!

Here's what happened: _____

_____

_____

_____

8

You'll never believe what happened on

Thursday. A _____

came to my birthday party! _____

_____

_____

_____

6

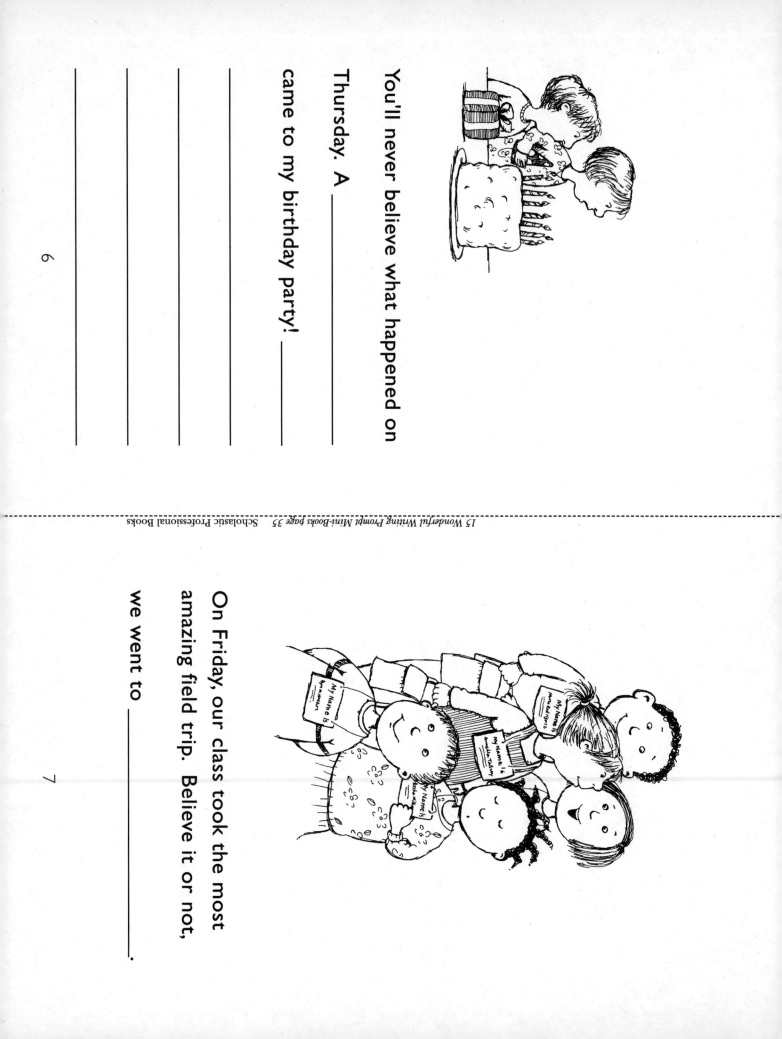

On Friday, our class took the most

amazing field trip. Believe it or not,

we went to _____

_____

7

Happy Valentine's Day!

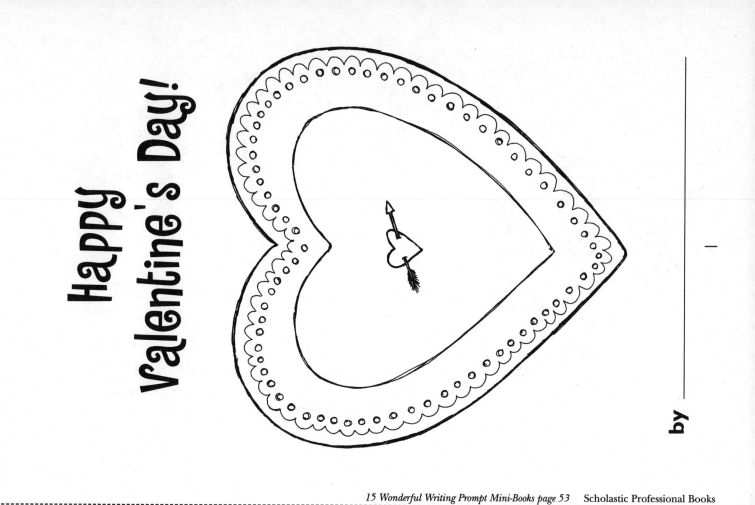

by _____

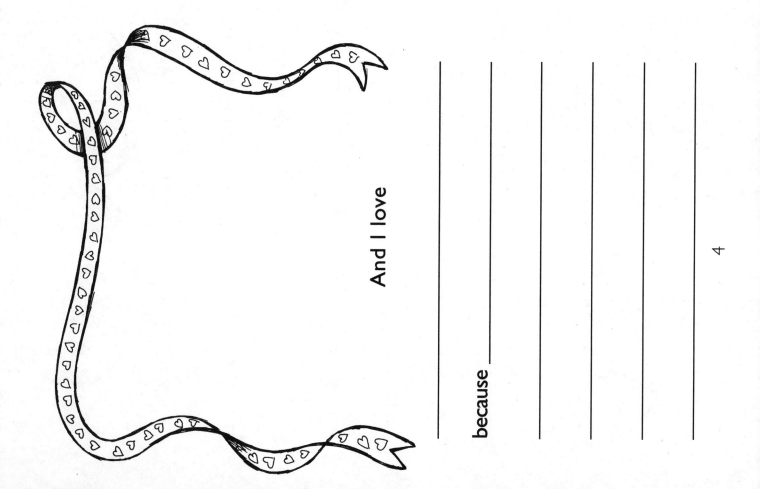

And I love

_____

because _____

_____

_____

_____

4

Happy Valentine's Day!

2

I love my

because

3

Look at what I wrote
on these candy hearts!

7

One of my favorite people in the whole

world is _____, because

_____

_____

_____

_____

6

The best thing about Valentine's Day is

8

I want to send a valentine to my friend

My friend is special because

5

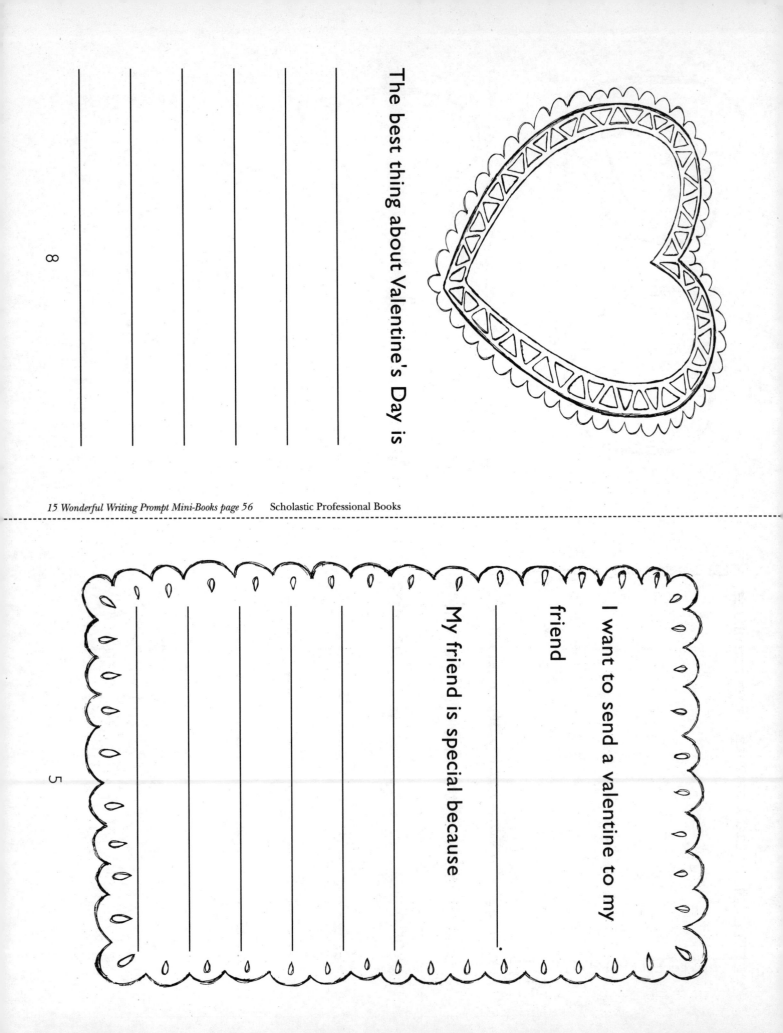

School Days

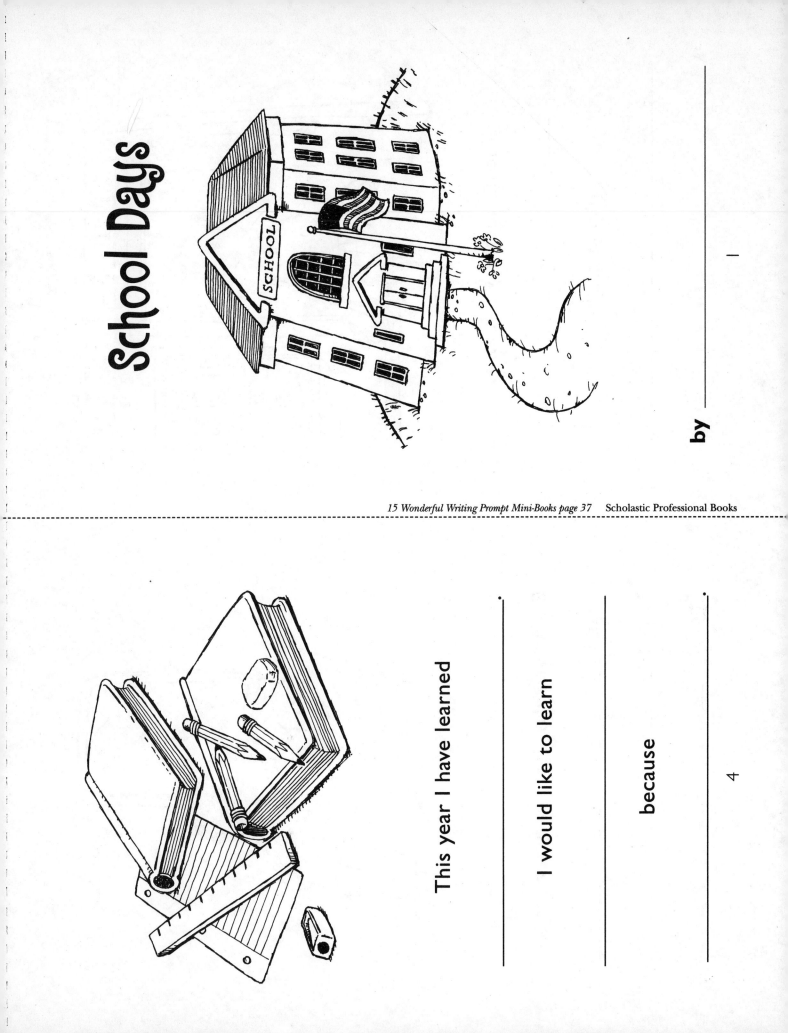

by _____

1

This year I have learned _____

I would like to learn _____

because _____

4

The name of my school is

_____

I'm in grade

_____

2

Every weekday I get ready for school.

First, I _____

Next, I _____

Then, I _____

3

One funny thing that happened at

school was

_____

_____

_____

_____

_____

7

A neat field trip we took was

_____

_____

_____

_____

_____

6

If I were principal for a day,

_____

_____

_____

_____

8

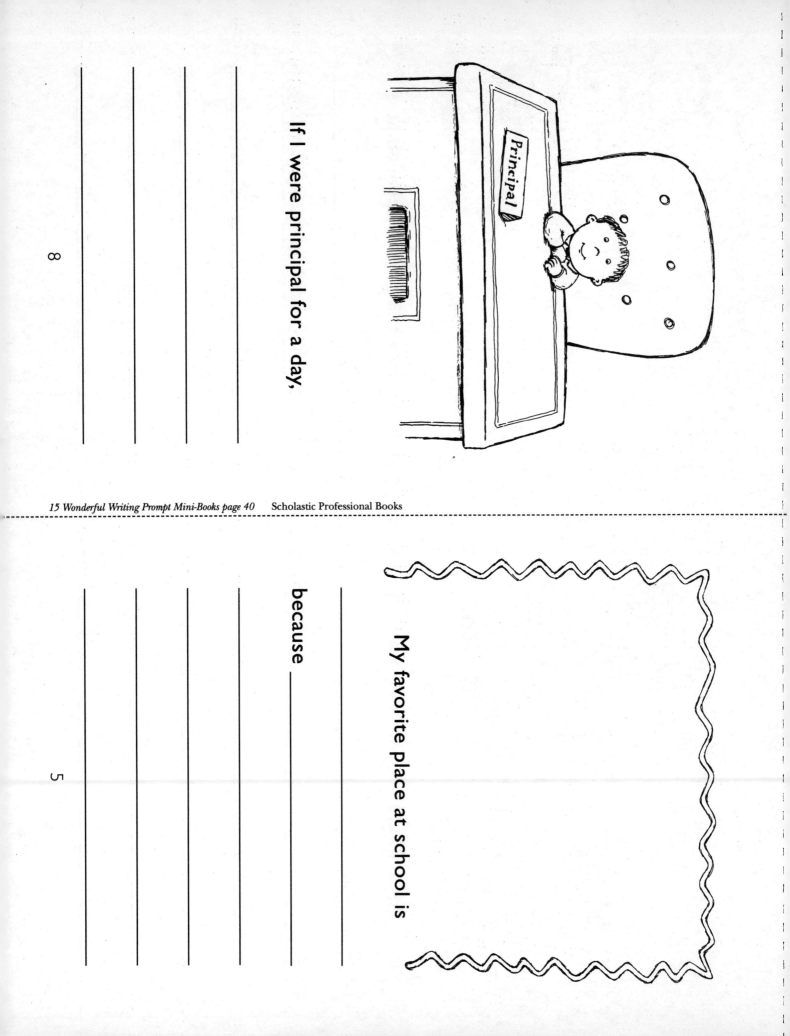

My favorite place at school is

because _____

_____

_____

_____

_____

5

The 100th Day of School

by _____

Would you rather live with 100 ants or 100 butterflies?

Why? _____
_____
_____
_____

4

Happy 100th day of school!
What would you choose if you could
have 100 of anything?

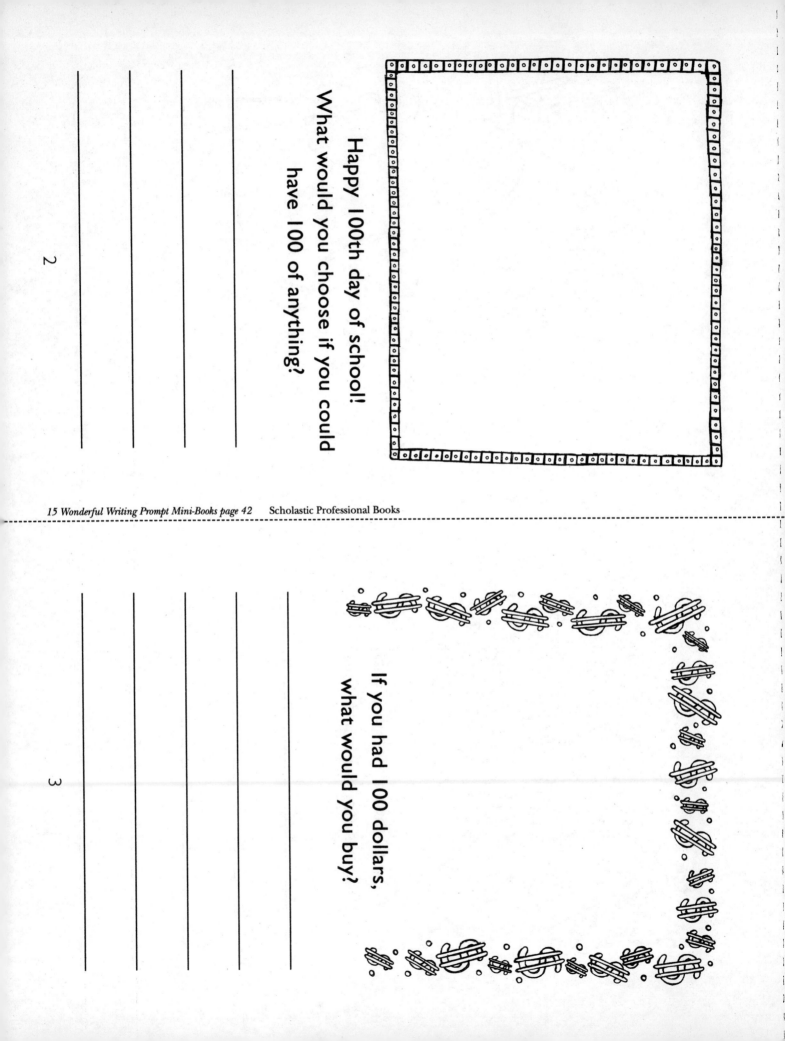

2

If you had 100 dollars,
what would you buy?

3

If you had to eat 100 of one sort of food, what would you choose to eat?

7

What could you do 100 times that would make you tired or sore?

6

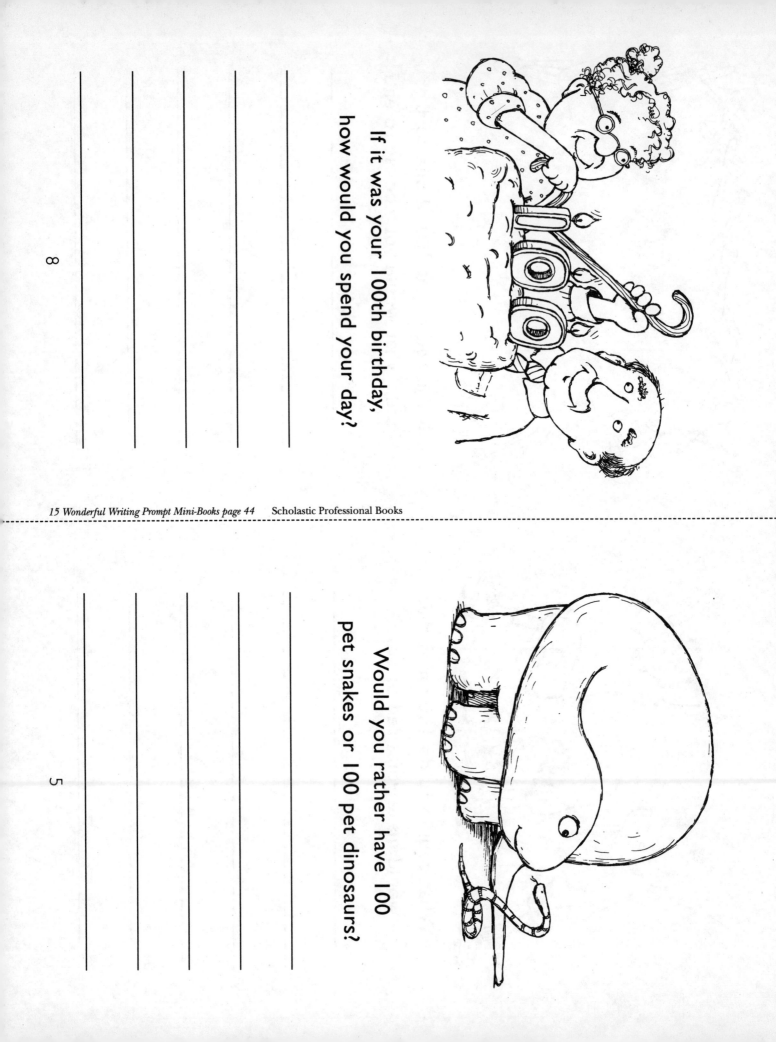

If it was your 100th birthday,
how would you spend your day?

8

Would you rather have 100
pet snakes or 100 pet dinosaurs?

5

The Lonely Giant

by _____

1

Whenever he went to a restaurant,

_____
_____
_____
_____
_____

4

Once upon a time, there was a very lonely giant. He was lonely because

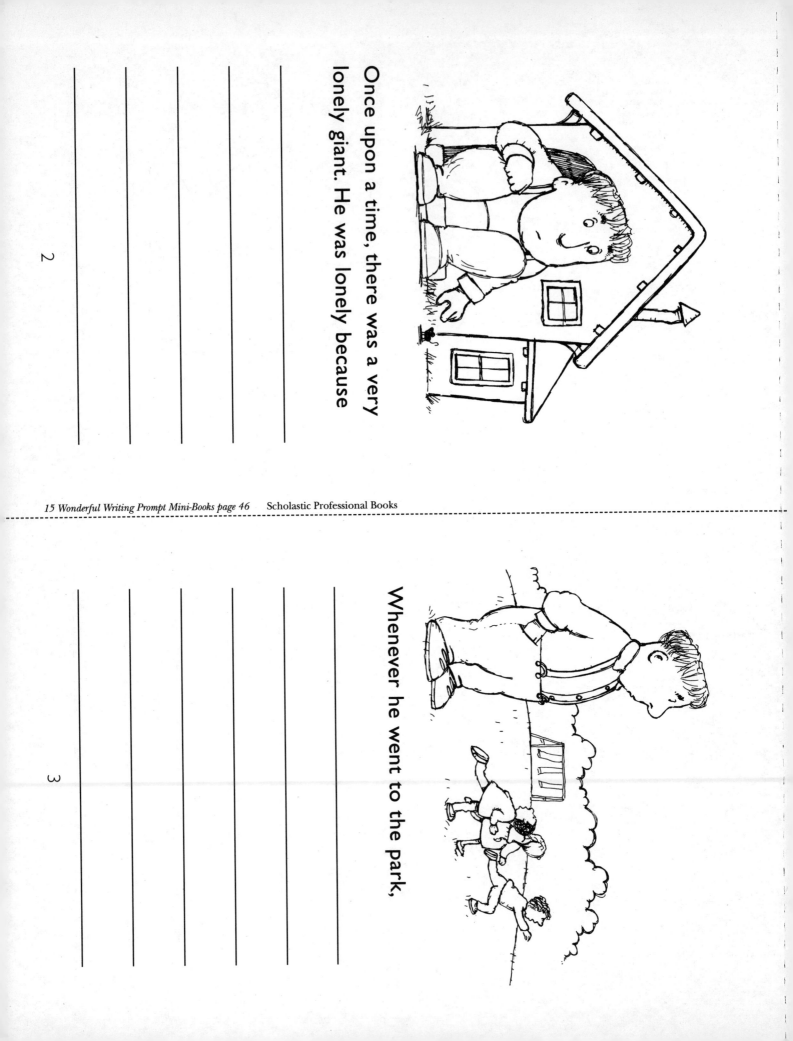

2

Whenever he went to the park,

3

From that day on, _____

_____

_____

_____

_____

7

Then one day, _____

_____

_____

_____

_____

6

About the Author:

8

The giant was so sad. He said to himself,

5

My Words of Wisdom

by _____

1

Dear Big Bad Wolf,

Everyone thinks you're the bad guy.

Here's what you could do to have more friends: _____

_____

_____

_____

_____

_____

4

Dear Cinderella,
I see you are very sad. Here's what you should do: _____

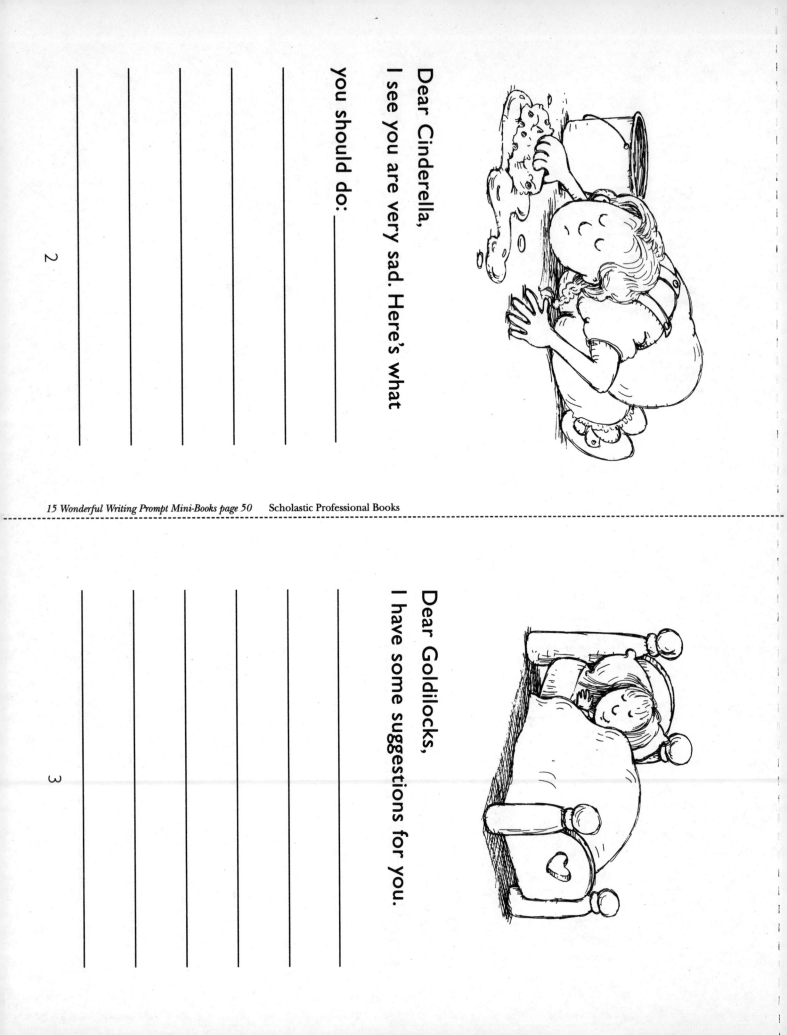

2

Dear Goldilocks,
I have some suggestions for you.

3

Dear Jack,

If I were you, I would _____

_____

_____

_____

_____

_____

_____

_____

7

Dear Little Red Riding Hood,

If I were you, I would _____

_____

_____

_____

_____

_____

_____

6

Dear _____,

_____

8

Dear Hansel and Gretel,
Next time you're lost in the woods,

5

The best thing in my dream bedroom would be

_____.

It would be fun to have it because _____

_____

_____

_____

_____

5

The book character I would be friends with is

_____.

We would _____

_____

_____

_____

_____

4

One last thing! In my dream world, I would

_____

_____

_____

_____

_____

8

My Dream World

by _____

I

My dream pet would
be a _____.

It would _____

_____

_____

_____

3

On my dream
vacation I would go to

_____.

I would _____

_____

_____

_____

6

In my dream world,
I would be _____
years old. Then I could

_____

_____

_____

draw in your candles

2

At my dream school,

_____

_____

_____

_____

_____

_____

7

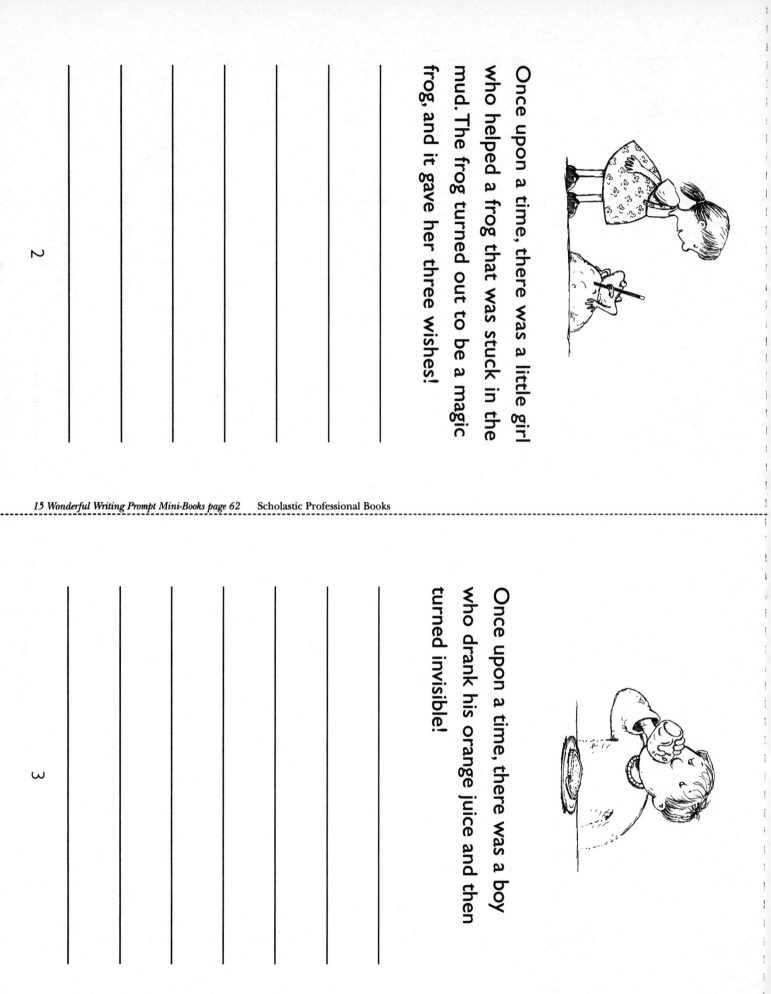

Once upon a time, there was a little girl who helped a frog that was stuck in the mud. The frog turned out to be a magic frog, and it gave her three wishes!

2

Once upon a time, there was a boy who drank his orange juice and then turned invisible!

3

My Very Own Folk and Fairy Tales

by _____

Did you ever wonder why the elephant has such a long trunk? The elephant started out with a very small nose, but

_____

_____

_____

_____

4

About the Author

7

Do you know why the leopard has

spots? It's because _____

6

8

Once upon a time, there was a boy who wished he had some brothers and sisters. Instead, he woke up one morning to find twelve elves in his room! He _____

5